GRADE 2

The Syllabus of Examination requirements, especially tho sight-reading. Attention sho Notices on the inside front cc of any changes.

The syllabus is obtainable fro The Associated Board of the ......chools of Music, 24 Portland Place, London W1B 1LU (please send a stamped addressed C5 (162mm × 229mm) envelope).

In examination centres outside the UK, information and syllabuses may be obtained from the Local Representative.

CONTENTS

page

LIST A

1   **Thomas Campion** (1567–1620) Fain would I wed, arr. Edward Huws Jones — 2
2   **Johann Christoph Pepusch** (1667–1752) Largo in D: Sonata in B minor, Op. 2 No. 7, third movement — 3
3   **Georg Philipp Telemann** (1681–1767) Gavotte, from *The Fashionable Dilettante Damon* — 4

LIST B

1   **Edward Elgar** (1857–1934) Andantino in G, No. 4 from *Very Easy Melodious Exercises in the First Position*, Op. 22 — 5
2   **I. Negely** Pastorale — 6
3   **L. Liubovski** Ancient Dance — 7

LIST C

1   **Richard Rodney Bennett** A Quiet Conversation, No. 4 from *Up Bow, Down Bow* — 8
2   **Katherine and Hugh Colledge** Coconuts and Mangoes, No. 14 from *Shooting Stars* — 9
3   **Peter Martin** Jig, No. 3 from Little Suite No. 4 — 10

Where appropriate, pieces in this volume have been checked with original source material and edited as necessary for instructional purposes. Fingering, phrasing, bowing, metronome marks and the editorial realization of ornaments (where given) are for guidance but are not comprehensive or obligatory.

DO NOT PHOTOCOPY © MUSIC

Alternative pieces for this grade

LIST A

4   **Mozart** Minuet, K. 94. No. 9 from *A First Book of Classical and Romantic Pieces*, arr. Forbes (OUP)
5   **J. J. Walther** Aria, from Suite No. 19 in B flat. *Baroque Violin Pieces*, Book 1, ed. Jones (Associated Board)
6   **Purcell** Symphony, from *King Arthur*. No. 1 from Purcell, *Easy Pieces for Violin and Piano*, arr. Nagy (Universal/MDS)

LIST B

4   **Walter Carroll** Singhalese Dancer, No. 10 from *The Enchanted Isle* (Forsyth)
5   **Schubert** Berceuse, from D. 946/2. No. 15 from *A First Book of Classical and Romantic Pieces*, arr. Forbes (OUP)
6   **Tchaikovsky** Waltz, from *Sleeping Beauty*. *Superpieces 2*, arr. Cohen (Faber)

LIST C

4   **Anon.** The four corners of my handkerchief (*with violin melody line*). *The Gypsy Fiddler*, arr. Huws Jones (Boosey & Hawkes)
5   **Anon. Irish** Star of the County Down (*with violin melody line*). *The Ceilidh Collection*, arr. Huws Jones (Boosey & Hawkes)
6   **Hilary Burgoyne** Chicken Reel, No. 19 from *Take the Stage* (Boosey & Hawkes)

Music origination by Jack Thompson.
Cover by Økvik Design.
Printed in England by Halstan & Co. Ltd, Amersham, Bucks.

Fain would I wed

Arranged by
Edward Huws Jones

CAMPION

Fain would I wed is from Thomas Campion's *Fourth Booke of Ayres* published in 1617 or 1618. The melody is based on a popular chord sequence known as the 'passamezzo antico' – also found in *Greensleeves.* EHJ

Largo in D

Third Movement from Sonata in B minor, Op. 2 No. 7

Edited by
Richard Jones

PEPUSCH

The violin part, which is akin to a slow, stately dance tune, contrasts with the continuous tread of the 'walking-bass' accompaniment. The piece should be taken broadly, with generally long bow-strokes and expressive shaping of the phrases. Bowing (apart from that in bar 12), dynamics and articulation marks are editorial suggestions only.

Source: *Sonates à un violon seul & une basse continue*, Op. 2 (Amsterdam, 1707–8).

Gavotte

from *The Fashionable Dilettante Damon*

Transcribed and edited by
Richard Jones

TELEMANN

This is a shepherd's dance from Telemann's pastoral opera *Der neumodische Liebhaber Damon* (*The Fashionable Dilettante Damon*), which was first performed in Hamburg in 1724. The Gavotte was originally written for strings and the Trio for wind instruments. All dynamics and articulation marks are editorial suggestions only; the trill in bar 31 has also been added by the editor. In the original there is a trill in the melody on the first beat of bar 18.

Andantino in G

No. 4 from *Very Easy Melodious Exercises in the First Position*, Op. 22

ELGAR

This lovely melody needs a real sense of movement. The tempo must not be too slow or the bow can easily lose its flowing quality.

Reproduced by permission of Bosworth & Co. Ltd.
All enquiries for this piece apart from the examinations should be addressed to Bosworth & Co. Ltd, 8/9 Frith Street, London W1V 5TV.

B:2

Pastorale

NEGELY

Reproduced from *The Young Violinist's Repertoire,* Book 2 by permission. All enquiries for this piece apart from the examinations should be addressed to Faber Music Ltd, 3 Queen Square, London WC1N 3AU.

Ancient Dance

B:3

LIUBOVSKI

AB 2746

A Quiet Conversation

No. 4 from *Up Bow, Down Bow*

RICHARD RODNEY BENNETT

Reproduced by permission of Novello & Co. Ltd.
All enquiries for this piece apart from the examinations should be addressed to Novello & Co. Ltd, 8/9 Frith Street, London W1V 5TV.

Coconuts and Mangoes

No. 14 from *Shooting Stars*

KATHERINE and
HUGH COLLEDGE

C:2

C:3

Jig

No. 3 from Little Suite No. 4

PETER MARTIN

Checklist of Scales and Arpeggios

Candidates and teachers may find this checklist useful in learning the requirements of the grade. Full details of the forms of the various requirements, including details of rhythms, starting notes and bowing patterns, are given in the syllabus and in the scale books published by the Board.

Grade 2

			separate bows					slurred					
								two quavers to a bow					
Major Scales	**C Major**	1 Octave											
	F Major	1 Octave											
	G Major	2 Octaves											
	A Major	2 Octaves											
	B♭ Major	2 Octaves											
								two quavers to a bow					
Minor Scales *(melodic or harmonic)*	**G Minor**	1 Octave											
	D Minor	1 Octave											
	A Minor	1 Octave											
								not applicable					
Major Arpeggios	**C Major**	1 Octave											
	F Major	1 Octave											
	G Major	2 Octaves											
	A Major	2 Octaves											
	B♭ Major	2 Octaves											
								not applicable					
Minor Arpeggios	**G Minor**	1 Octave											
	D Minor	1 Octave											
	A Minor	1 Octave											